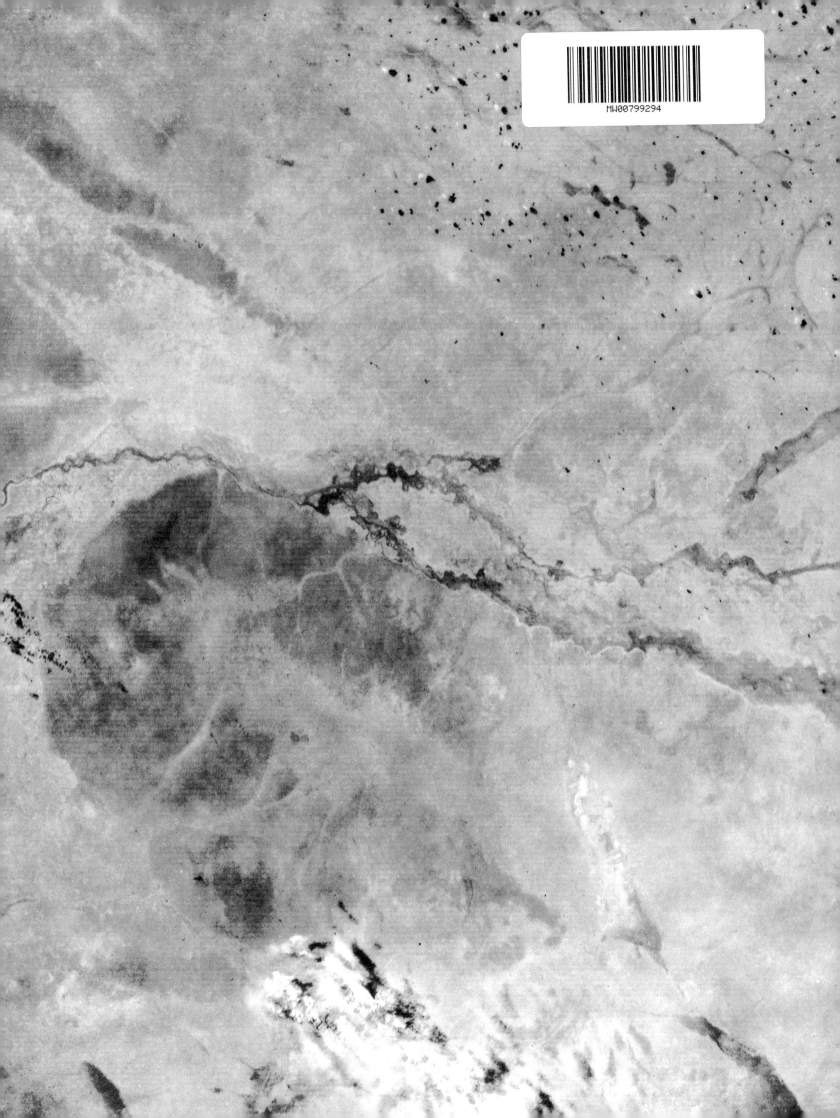

Fazal Sheikh

A Sense of Common Ground

Scalo Zurich – Berlin – New York

My first trip to the Sudanese refugee camp on Kenya's northwestern border with the Sudan, in June of 1992, was aboard a United Nations High Commission for Refugees (UNHCR) flight from Nairobi. Though nearly four years ago, the trip remains vivid in my mind and has informed the way that I have documented Africa's refugee communities since.

There were ten of us on the plane: aid workers, two journalists and one cameraman. Before embarking on the journey we were briefed on what we were about to witness. From the cool and comfort of Nairobi it was difficult to imagine the harsh and remote terrain of the northern desert. The United Nations Public Affairs Officer spoke in hushed tones about the 25,000 refugees in the camp. In particular, he lingered on the "facts" concerning the "Unaccompanied Minors".

These "Unaccompanied Minors" were a group of nearly 12,000 boys between the ages of eight and eighteen who had been taken from southern Sudan to neighboring Ethiopia to be "taught." The implication was that the boys had been abducted by members of the Sudanese People's Liberation Army (SPLA) and had been taken to Ethiopia where they were trained as soldiers for later deployment in the war against the Islamic dominated Sudanese government. With the fall of the Ethiopian government in 1991, the Sudanese were forced to return to southern Sudan on foot. When the Sudanese government forces defeated the SPLA in the battle for the southern town of Kapoeta, the boys fled, once again by foot, into northern Kenya. The United Nations spokesman hinted at the manipulation of the "students" by the "teachers". Catchwords like "manipulation", "orphan", "Unaccompanied Minor", "training", and "suffering" played in my mind as I boarded the plane for the north.

As soon as we landed on the sandy spit at Lokichoggio, the journalists began working. Their stories had to be compiled in hours as they were leaving in the afternoon on the return trip to Nairobi. As I watched them work throughout the day, I noticed they were drawn to the areas that the spokesman had suggested would provide the best footage. I had arranged to stay in the camp for several days and was under no pressure to begin working.

As I sat in the camp a few days after my arrival, I thought back to that first day and to my initial impressions about the camp, its residents and my role there. I realized that my early thoughts concerning the boys and their plight had been heavily influenced by what I had been told in the UNHCR briefing. I remembered watching the journalists working and feeling a sense of unease, an inability to follow along and make the expected photographs. Now, I moved about the village and the camp trying to make sense of the whirlwind in which I was engulfed.

I had been to this part of Africa several times before during trips to visit my family in Nairobi. During these periods, I had marvelled at the desolate stillness of the desert and the way in which it evoked a curious sensation of calm and solace mixed with a hint of foreboding. I thought back to those earlier times and I revisited some of the shopkeepers that I had met years before in an attempt to find some connection to the place I had once known.

As the days passed, and as I integrated my earlier experiences of the place with this new one, the preconceptions which had been foisted upon me in the initial briefing and the shock of the first encounter began to fade away, allowing a broader, expanded sense of the refugees and their situation to emerge. It was at this point that I began to ask the community elders and the refugees to collaborate with me in making the images.

Sudan 1992–1994

The Sudanese civil war between the Islamic dominated government and the Christian/Animist south, begun in 1983, has claimed an estimated 1.3 million lives in the past ten years. In the late 1980s hundreds of thousands of Sudanese fled into Ethiopia where they were given asylum by a Mengistu government sympathetic to the plight of the southern Sudanese. When the Ethiopian government fell in May of 1991, the Sudanese, including 17,000 "Unaccompanied Minors", were forced to flee in disarray back across the border to villages in southern Sudan. When the Sudanese town of Kapoeta was captured by the Sudanese government forces on May 19, 1992, the townspeople, many of whom had been in Ethiopia, fled once again, south to the town of Narus and on to the Kenyan border post at Lokichoggio. During the next two months the number of refugees at the Lokichoggio "transit center" swelled to 25,000. By the end of July 1992 the UNHCR had already begun transporting the residents of the transit camp to a more permanent and secure settlement at Kakuma, Kenya. In November of 1995 the Kakuma refugee camp was home to 41,665 Sudanese of which 7,000 were Unaccompanied Minors.

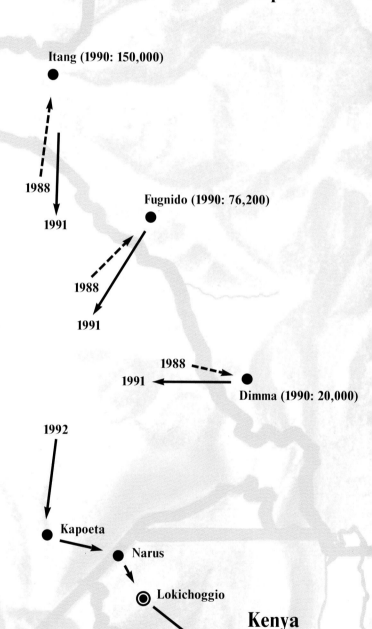

Ethiopia

Itang (1990: 150,000)

1988

1991

Fugnido (1990: 76,200)

1988

1991

1988

1991

Dimma (1990: 20,000)

1992

Kapoeta

Narus

Lokichoggio

Kenya

Kakuma
(Nov. 1995: 41,700)

Adjumani

Arua

Uganda
(1995: 200,000)

Rachel (left) and Ochol, Lokichoggio

Akuot Nyibol (pregnant at center) with Riak Warabek (right) and Akuot's daughter, Athok Duom, who is recovering from malaria, Lokichoggio.

"Teacher" (left) and "student" (Unaccompanied Minor), Kakuma

Sudanese mountains in the distance

Peter Shan (Unaccompanied Minor), Kakuma

Loading trucks for journey to refugee camp at Kakuma

Lokichoggio "transit center"

Dawn at Lokichoggio

Deng's cousin, mortar amputee, Lokichoggio

Moving south

Presenting tin airplane

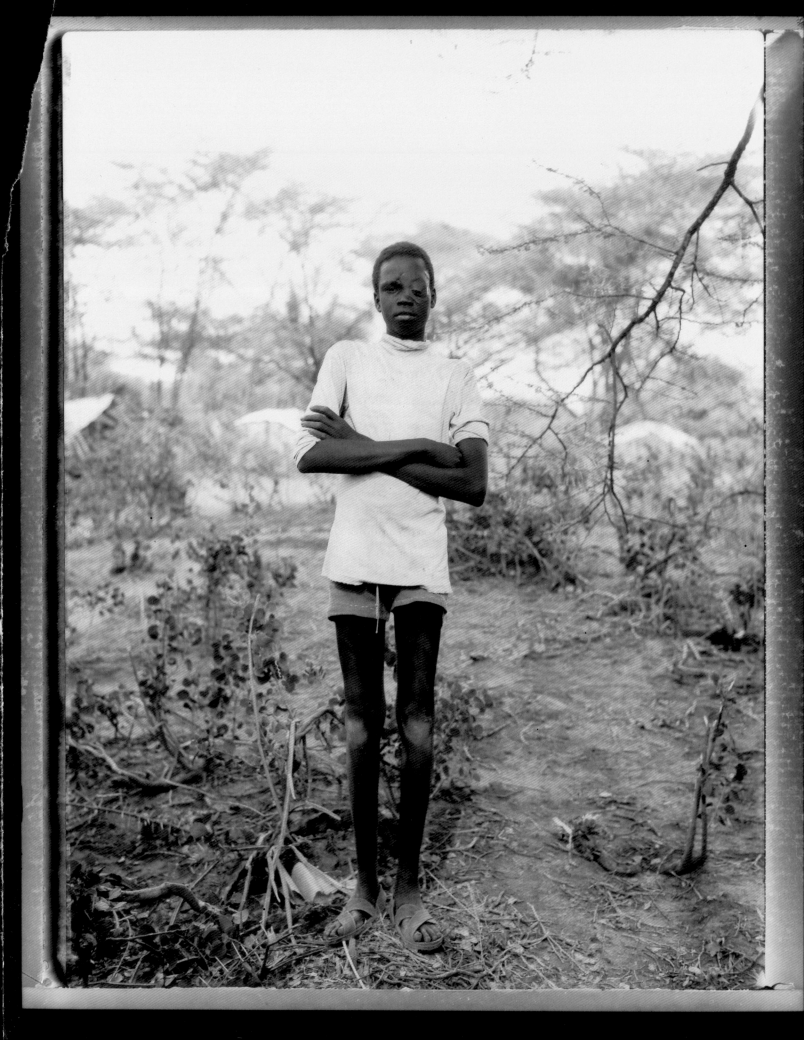

Daniel Ajak (Unaccompanied Minor), rescued as an infant from hyena abduction by Dinka neighbors, Kakuma.

William Gai (left) and Peter Deng (Unaccompanied Minors), Lokichoggio

Unaccompanied Minors, Kakuma

Mabout (left) and Thou Deng with UN Landrover

Brother and sister

Joseph (left) and Peter

Marior models handmade glasses

Anthill

Alang with Dinka elder

David

Gabriel (left), Madang (center), and Peter

Mawout Yuot

Agai Miriam Adeng (Unaccompanied Minor), Kakuma

Final approach to refugee camp at Kakuma; today twelve boys arrived on foot from Juba.

William Biar Gai (left) and Bol Aguot (Unaccompanied Minors), Kakuma

Kai Chop Deng (Unaccompanied Minor) with handcrafted lyre (American relief aid oil can, sticks and wire), Kakuma

Ethiopia 1992 – 1993

The Ethiopian refugee camp at Walda, Kenya, established in August of 1991, was initially home to 9,500 urban refugees who had fled Ethiopia in the period following the fall of the Mengistu regime in May of 1991. In the beginning of 1992, tribal clashes in the rural south of Ethiopia broke out between the Gari and Borana tribes. The effects of the clashes, exacerbated by a severe drought, caused a mass exodus from the south of Ethiopia toward the Kenyan border posts at Sololo and Moyale. In the following weeks, the population of the Ethiopian refugee camp at Walda soared to over 50,000 as Ethiopians arrived on foot from the border regions. The Gari and Borana tribal members in the camp, reflecting on the traditional harmony between the two tribes, referred to the clashes as the "family war." Towards the end of 1992, the warring parties in southern Ethiopia signed a peace accord which enabled the UNHCR to begin a repatriation campaign. In the early months of 1993, the majority of Walda's refugees voluntarily repatriated to their home villages. Those who refused to return were transferred to other camps in northern Kenya. On April 15, 1993 the Ethiopian refugee camp at Walda, Kenya was closed.

Addis Ababa

1991

Ethiopia

Sidamo Province

1992

Gofa Province 1992

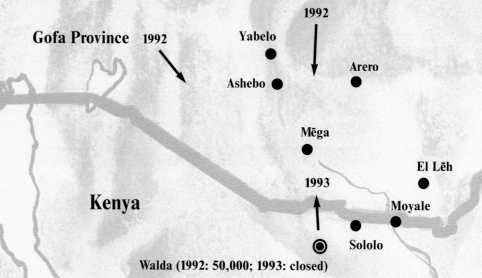

Yabelo

Ashebo

Arero

Mēga

El Lēh

1993

Moyale

Kenya

Sololo

Walda (1992: 50,000; 1993: closed)

Gulma Duba Salo, Borana elder from Arero

Gari widow, Faduma Hussein Isat at 70 years old walked from El Lēi with her five children to the Kenyan border post at Moyale.

Stork flies over

Gabbra tribal matriarch

The main problems of Borona Tribes

The Transitional Government of Ethiopia EPDRF with
Their followers accomplices Geri. Gabera. Guji and Tegree
Tribes had been fighting against borona tribes in ethiopia by—
Burning their houses, looting their properties, Killing and arresting
The borona people who were living in ethiopia

These borona tribes were detested and killed by tegree
Government of ethiopia, because of they are oromo people in tribe
and oromo-liberation front - O.L.F are contrary to the interests of
EPDRF. there by they looted borona people like the previous regimes
and supporters of O.L.F. hence the borona tribes became enemy
OF EPDRF In ethiopia

For Example: the under named borona people head leaders
Those who were arrested by tegree EPDRF in ethiopia

1· BULEE KULU GUYO 2· GOLISA ROBA 3· DAWID DABASU
These three persons are still imprisoned in ethiopia and they
are going to be killed by tegree / EPDRF

most of the borona people because of all these above mentioned
problems they fled to kenya to save their lives and camped here
In Walda refugees camp. since the time they settled here in
Walda the problems that they had been frightened when they were
In ethiopia come with and following after them to kenya, walda
Refugees camp and nirobi

For Example:- The man whose name is called Jahatani
Ali tandu who was the famous and head leader of borona people
was killed by EPDRF and Geri spies on 2/6/92 in nirobi

Here in walda from borona tribes refugees about eight (8)
persons were killed, 12 persons were disappeared, ten (10) persons were
wounded by Geri tribel refugees on 29/7/92

ALL the deadsmen bodies were maimed to pieces and thrown
away. when this accedent happened to borona tribes ten (10) other
Tribes who are in walda as arefugee from different country, UNHCR
of walda, and walda police station were eyewitness for the above
mentioned conditions. thereby if we think to goback to ethiopia we
will not able to get peace. for our problems are still going on in ethiopia.

From now on here in walda camp we can't stay for long time
for we have been suffering and in fatal conditions

Hence we would like to report you as soon as possible
as you try to give us solution which will satisfy us and protect
us from all our above mentioned problems.

We do hope as you will give us aposetive
answer. We beg and ask you all above mentioned
problems to get solution within few days   with Thanks.

Letter given to me by the Borana elders of Walda in August of 1992   Bashia Gababo Sharamu, Borana elder from Yabelo

Borana War widows Tumia Bonia Huka (left) and Darmi Roba Kosi left Gofa province together when their husbands
were killed in an early morning raid by Gari attackers.

Borana war widow Darmi Halake Gilo walked from Ashebo to the Kenyan border post at Sololo.

Maribou storks on shared burial site

Gari war widow Kairoi Boru Wano

Ethiopian mountains in the distance

Aisha, one week before repatriation

Path to refugee camp at Walda

Orthodox Church

Somalia 1992 – 1994

The tribal and clan-based clashes which began in Somalia in 1991 soon spread to the Kenyan border regions. The initial exodus from Somalia into Kenya was to the town of Liboi, where a camp was quickly erected in January of 1991. In December of 1992, Liboi had a population of 45,000 refugees. Fighting broke out in the region near Mandera on April 28, 1992 and the town, which saw a border site quickly fashioned, witnessed an influx which amounted to 55,000 by the end of 1992. At the height of the emergency in 1992 there were 500,000 Somali refugees living in Kenyan camps. Under pressure from the Kenyan government to stem the tide of refugees, the UNHCR began a cross border operation to pave the way for Somalis to return to their homes. On April 15, 1994 Mandera border site was closed and those Somalis not willing to return home were moved south to the camp at Dadaab. On June 17, 1994 Liboi refugee camp experienced the same fate. As the uncertainty concerning the future of Somalia continues, the consolidation of the Somali communities is complete and the remaining 103,667 Somali refugees who continue to resist repatriation efforts remain in the camps surrounding Dadaab.

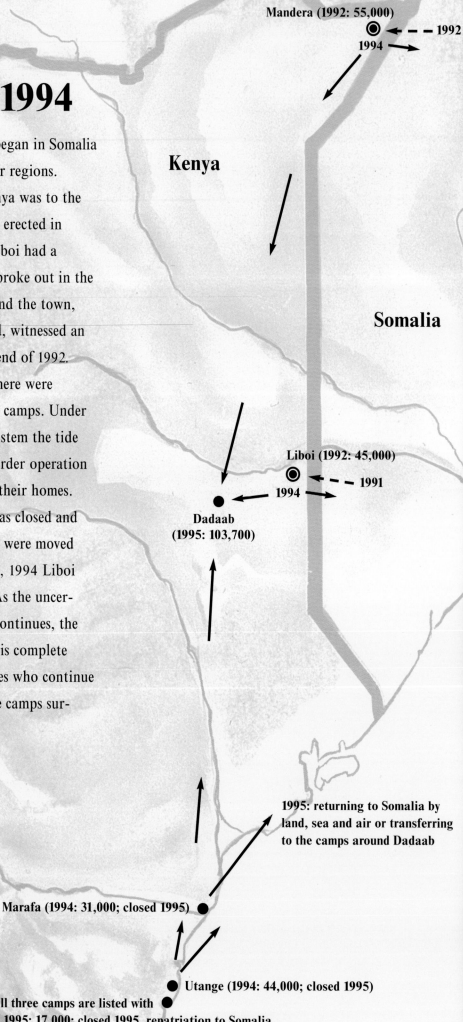

Mandera (1992: 55,000)
1992
1994

Kenya

Somalia

Liboi (1992: 45,000)
1994   1991

Dadaab
(1995: 103,700)

1995: returning to Somalia by land, sea and air or transferring to the camps around Dadaab

Marafa (1994: 31,000; closed 1995)

Utange (1994: 44,000; closed 1995)

Jomvu, Hatimi, Swaleh Nguru (All three camps are listed with one mark on the map. 1995: 17,000; closed 1995, repatriation to Somalia, movement to Dadaab and 1,000 members of the Benadir clan to be resettled to the United States)

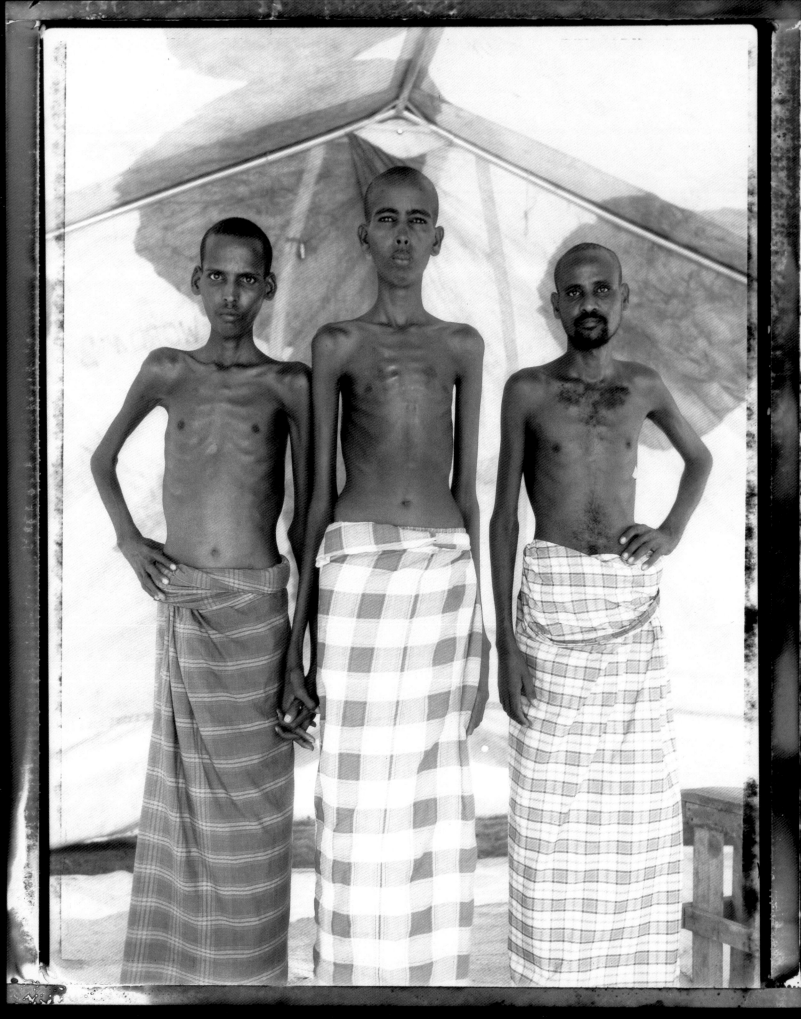

Mohamed Omar Gudle (left), Hussein Dahir Hassan (at center), and Abdul Rehman Ibrahim (miracle recovery patient), tuberculosis ward, Mandera

Since we were in Liboi as a refuggee, we have been Living here for four years. When we arrived in Kenya we were welcomed warmly by Kenya Governement and UNHCR addition to NGOs. We are very grate full for that. During the settelment of this camp (was very hard work with so many difficulties and problems. The died people were atleast 500 persons;

Luckifully, The humanitarian organization and Kenya Govreement shown all efforts and succeeded such as water, Sanitation, Health, security and food. (As a emmergency.) After wards. The refuggee people has adopted the Liboi satiuation to make the means of life. For example, shelter, Toilets, Dugsis for Quran. schools, mosgaus, Kichens, Shadows, small bussiness, on so on. Fortunately. Diseases and mortality has decreases for 80% -

→ After that we recieved an information from UNHCR office Liboi; Telling that, The refuggees comp Liboi will remove to DADAB/ Ifo. In the coming months. We discussed about this, we said its unacceptiable The reasons with our decision are these below:—

P. T. O. ——→

1- First of all, We request from kenya authorities ~~out labor~~ and UNHCR to leave us for our position Liboi, untill Our countery tobe quite normal.

2- If it is negative, We are not ready to DADAB/IFO. Tottaly.

3- We are sure or bleive. ~~Figes~~ to remove to Ifo is like The way of death. becouse of its more dangerous Than the flee of civil war for which brought us here.

4- We have made here every thing which is essential for human life. (security, Health, Water ETc)

5- We Sure that in Ifo There is Rape case, Bandates but not in Liboi since 1992.

6- We request again and again to leave us as we are now or to respect The previous Repatration.

7- All in all we are quite eager to repatriate to our countery due to The Nairobi agreement in this We would like to be Patient since the final solution of our countery. Otherwise we object for removal

Refugees committees ~~and~~ and Elders.

Mahled Khalif Ali, Farah Abdulla Mahied, Mohles olow Arays. Omar Haret Hirey, Hussein Abdi Ali, Ali Hassan Husseen. Aden Abdi Gass, Mohlud Abdi Madar. Osman Hussein Abdullahi, Mahled Ali Dhabbar. Abdullahi Bihi Amen

by: Kalakaam

Mahmoud Abdi Madir

Abdi Mohamed Omar

Mohamed Olow Ali

Mohamed Ali Dabar

Refugee Chairman Mohamed Khalif Ali

Hussein Abdi Ali

Mohamed Abdi Chama

Abdullai Bihi Amaz and his first wife Rukia Ali Ismael

Mohamed Ali Dabar and his granddaughter Nimo Mohamed

Somali elder's son, Mohamed Abdi Gas

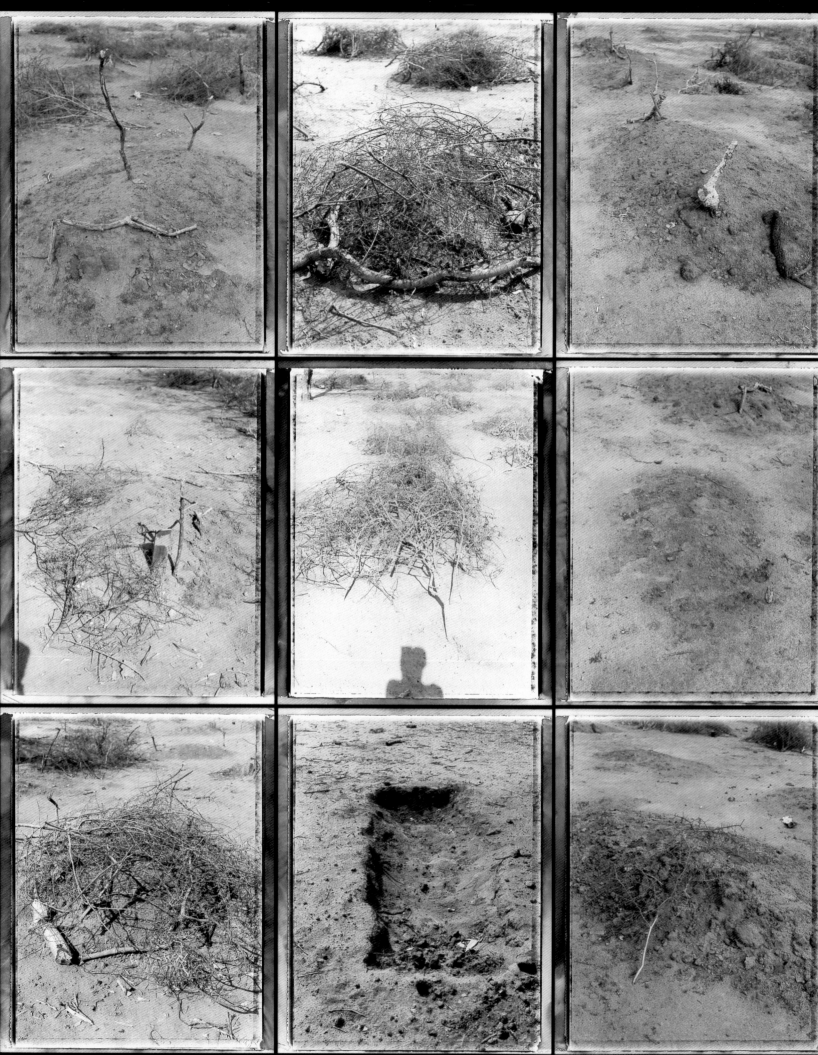

One evening in 1993 I sat talking with a Kenyan doctor in his compound at the Mandera border site. During our conversation, he spoke of the incidence of Somali nomad families from the border region smothering their malnourished infants. The days following my discussion with this doctor I spent at the Médecins Sans Frontières feeding center for children below 60 percent of total body weight. These children, close to 50 in number, were brought to the center twice daily by a parent or sibling who stayed with the child throughout the day, administering the prescribed treatment. It was the doctor's belief that the smotherings were easily explained by noting the essentially callous and aggressive nature of Somalis.

Shamsa Moka Abdi (left) and her sister Shahil

Harira Abdullai Mohamoud and her son Mohamed

Fatuma Adan and her daughter Abiba

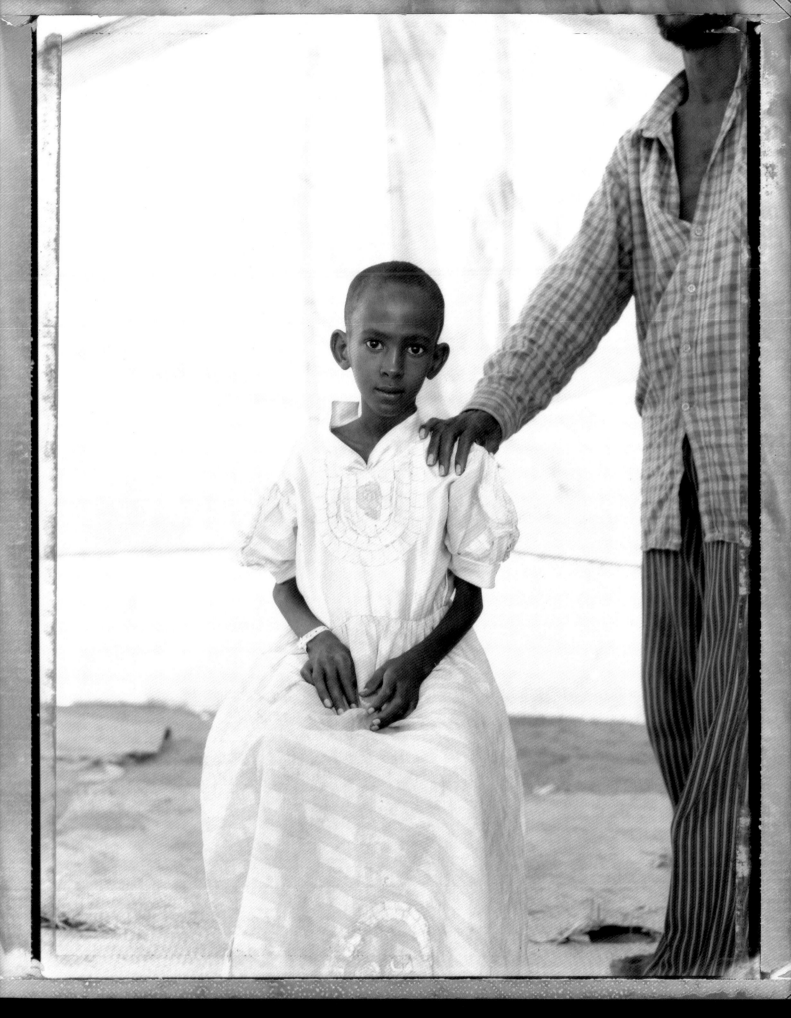

Hadija and her father. Eight year old Hadija remains mute after being separated from her mother in the crossing from Somalia into Kenya.

Mozambique 1994

On June 25, 1975, after ten years of insurrection, Mozambique gained independence from the Portuguese who had ruled their country for 400 years. By March of 1976 the country was plunged into civil war between the government forces of the Frente de Libertacao de Mozambique (FRELIMO) and the rebel movement of Resistencia Nacional Mozambicana (RENAMO). The fifteen-year civil war, exacerbated by recurrent droughts, caused an estimated 1.7 million Mozambicans to seek refuge in six neighboring countries. On October 4, 1992 a peace agreement was signed between FRELIMO and RENAMO, putting an end to the civil war. The UNHCR then began the largest repatriation campaign ever undertaken. In 1995, as Mozambicans returned to their homes, Nyamithuthu and the other refugee camps in Malawi, which had been home to more than 1,000,000 refugees, were closed.

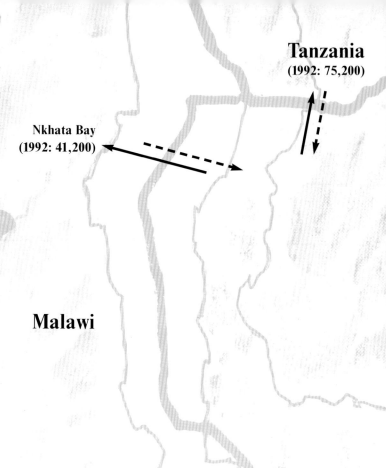

Tanzania
(1992: 75,200)

Nkhata Bay
(1992: 41,200)

Malawi

Lilongwe (1993: 32,300)

Dedza (1993: 139,900)

Mangoche (1993: 40,700)

Ncheu (1993: 132,000)

All camps in Malawi were closed by June 1995 with the refugees returning to their homes.

Mozambique

Mwanza (1993: 134,100)

Thyolo (1993: 25,600)

Chikwawa (1993: 94,000)

Milange (1993: 56,200)

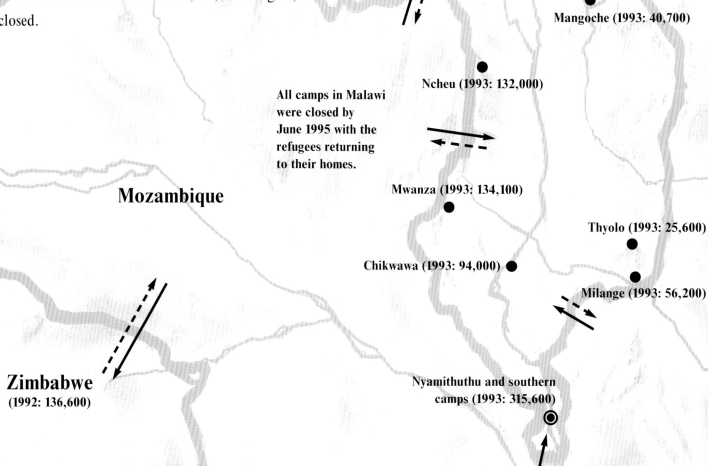

Zimbabwe
(1992: 136,600)

Nyamithuthu and southern camps (1993: 315,600)

Zambia (1992: 26,300); Swaziland (1992: 48,100); South Africa (1992: 250,000)

Traditional birthing attendant Chasasa Mahdi (right) with Raura Juao and her newborn daughter Shika

Mozambican elder Juaqui Tenfar (left) with section leader Juao Thom

Section leader Faria Antonio (right) with Mozambican elder Shik Thom

67

Midday meeting of Mozambican elders to discuss repatriation

Rwanda 1994

On April 6, 1994 the plane carrying President
Habyarimana of Rwanda and President Ntaryamira of
Burundi was shot down as it approached Kigali airport
and both men were killed. The event sparked ethnic
clashes between Rwanda's Hutu and Tutsi that have left
hundreds of thousands dead. On April 29, 1994 the
largest and swiftest exodus of refugees in the history of
refugee migration occurred as 250,000 Rwandans
flooded across the border into Tanzania in the course
of a single day. In the middle of July a further 500,000
fled across Rwanda's western border with Zaire. In
1995, the refugee camp at Lumasi was one of several
Rwandan camps on the Tanzanian side of the border
which are home to 583,000 Rwandan refugees as they
wait for the future of their country to unflold.

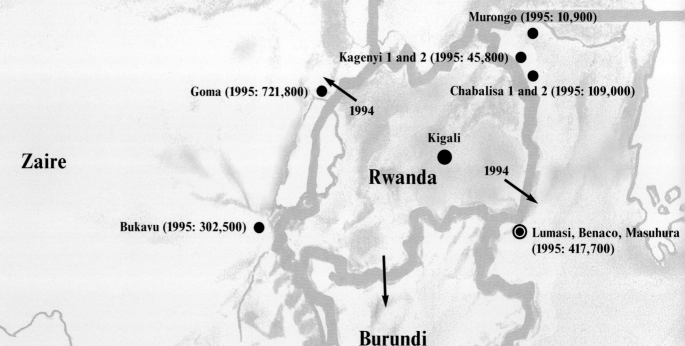

Uganda

Murongo (1995: 10,900)

Kagenyi 1 and 2 (1995: 45,800)

Goma (1995: 721,800)

Chabalisa 1 and 2 (1995: 109,000)

1994

Zaire

Kigali

Rwanda

1994

Bukavu (1995: 302,500)

Lumasi, Benaco, Masuhura
(1995: 417,700)

Burundi
(1995: 195,000)

Uvira (1995: 61,000)

Tanzania

Wezemana ("God is great") with her sleeping brother Mitonze

Lukelatabaru ("One who was born to make war") seated in front of the residents of his compound

Mukarukiza with her newborn Mukeshimana ("I have seen her because of God")

Traditional birthing attendant Nyirabahire Esteri holding newborns Nsabimana ("I beg something from God") and Mukanzabonimpa ("God will give me, but I do not know when") flanked by mothers Kanyange (left), Mukobatozi (right) and Mukobatozi's mother,

Ndimwabahari ("One who was born with milk and cattle") wounded by a Rwandan Patriotic Front bullet

Bigelegezo (left) and Mafieli

Umwogoshi Itimana Karimera ("God named") and Kaganda Jean Paul Choyanutseden (right)

Narame Fausta with her daughter Esther (left) and newborn Makantamba ("One who was born at the time of war")

Acknowledgements

A Sense of Common Ground was made possible by the elders and residents of the refugee communities from Sudan, Ethiopia, Somalia, Mozambique, and Rwanda who offered me their hospitality and instructed me in making these images. With the resolution of conflict and the signing of peace accords, many of these people have been able to return to their homes. For those still living in the refugee camps abroad, I wish for a swift resolution to conflict and peace.

I would also like to thank the following people and institutions for their support and encouragement:
Allan Albert, Vince Aletti, Charles and Cathy Ashmun, Lark Baxter, Virginia Beahan, William and Natalie Bland, Henry S. and Leigh Buchanan Bienen, Leslie Bienen, Peter C. Bunnell, Shaila Chaudry, Ellen Fitzpatrick, Emmet and Edith Gowin, Jodi Hauptman, Dr. Martin and Ellen Hauptman, Barbara Hitchcock and her efforts through the Polaroid Collection, Jeff Hoone and Light Work, Human Rights Watch and Jemera Rone, Mohamed Husain, Margaret Kannan, Peter MacGill, Deborah Gifford, Kim Jones and the entire staff at Pace Wildenstein MacGill, Médecins Sans Frontières, Belgium, France and Holland, Fausia Musse, Jeremiah P. Ostriker, The Princeton Materials Institute director Peter Eisenberger and manager Alexis Faust, Susan Rubenstein, Accra Shepp and Alva Rogers, Gerhard Steidl, Angelika and Fritz Stricker, Toshiko Takaezu, Carol Tate, Wood and Catherine Tate, UNHCR and its staff members Panos Moumtzis, Peter Kessler, Yusuf Hassan, and Millicent Mutuli, Johanna Wilson, Carla Williams, and Marciann Fallon for showing me strength and love.

To Walter Keller, for having faith in my work, and to Hans Werner Holzwarth of Design pur for his fresh perspective and gentle counsel.

I am grateful to Sam Yanes, Barbara Hitchcock and Polaroid Corporation for their continued support and sponsorship of the International Center for Photography exhibition, and to Miles Barth for his work on the traveling exhibition which accompanies this book.

And finally my deepest thanks to my family for giving their unconditional love and support. To my father and friend Abdul Majied Sheikh, and to his wife Seemin and her two children Fahd and Farrah, to Win and Lila Lenz who are sorely missed, to Robert, Sunny, Emily and Katie Lenz, to Libby Lenz, to Bill and Lisa Koutsoukos, to Zaidi and Zeba Sheikh, and to Gaby, Ali and Shela Sheikh.

Generous sponsorship for the creation of these images was provided by the National Endowment for the Arts, the New Jersey State Council on the Arts, the J. William Fulbright Foundation, and Polaroid Corporation.

The Publishers wish to thank the International Center for Photography, ICP, and Peter MacGill for their support.

Fazal Sheikh — A Sense of Common Ground

Design: Hans Werner Holzwarth, Design pur, Berlin | Production: Steidl, Göttingen

© 1996 for texts and photographs: Fazal Sheikh | © 1996 for this edition: Scalo Zurich – Berlin – New York,

Head Office: Weinbergstrasse 22a, CH-8001 Zurich/Switzerland, Phone 41 1 261 0910, Fax 41 1 261 9262

Distributed in North America by D.A.P., New York City; in Europe and Asia by Thames and Hudson, London

All rights reserved | First Scalo Edition, 1996 | ISBN 1-881616-51-7 | Printed in Germany

Endpapers: Satellite image of Kenya / Sudan border region (front); satellite image of Rwanda / Tanzania border region (back)